I0462619

SWEAR WORD COLORING BOOK FOR ADULTS

THIS BOOK BELONGS TO

____

First Printing, 2019

fuck you!

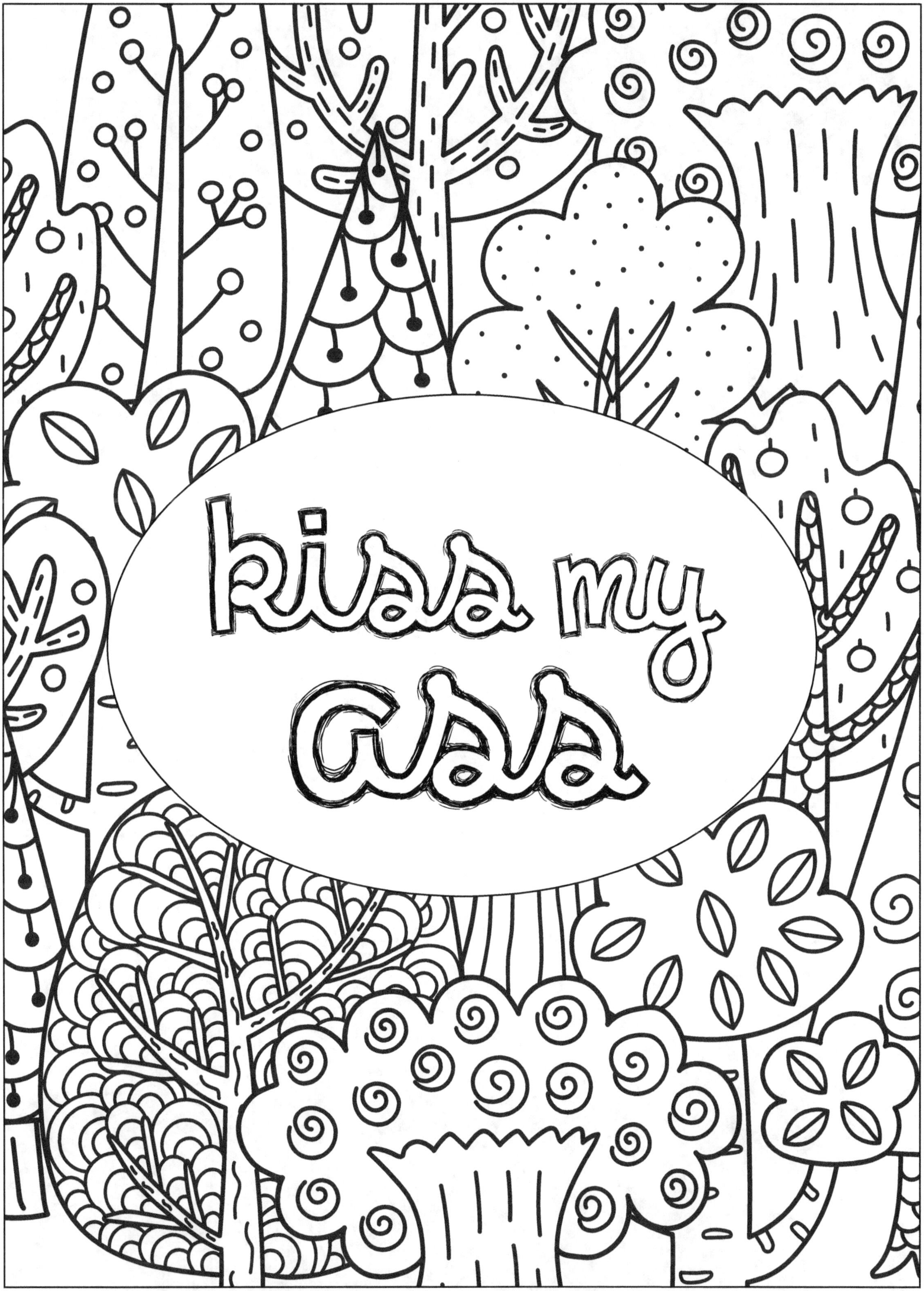
kiss my
ass

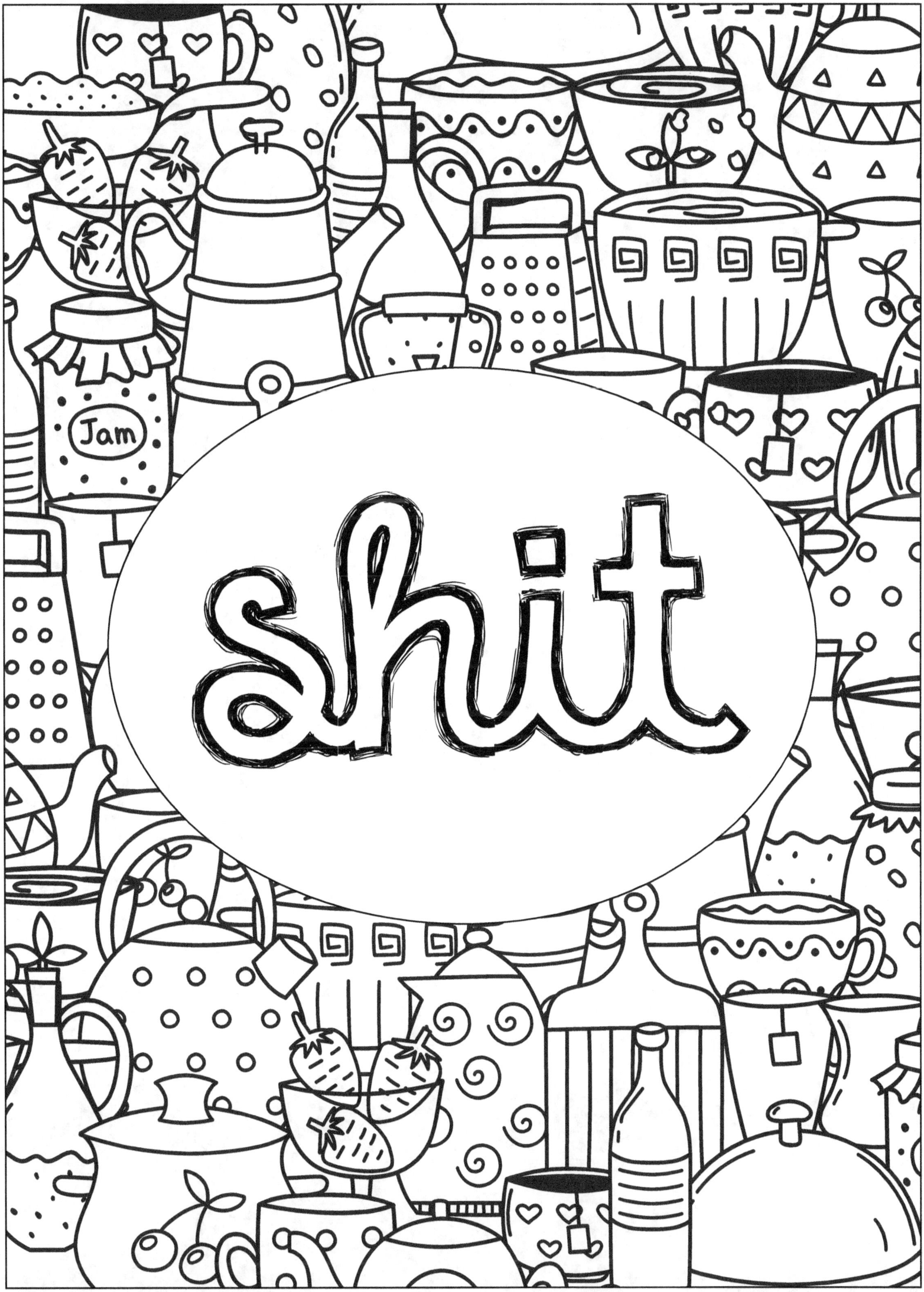
shit
Jam

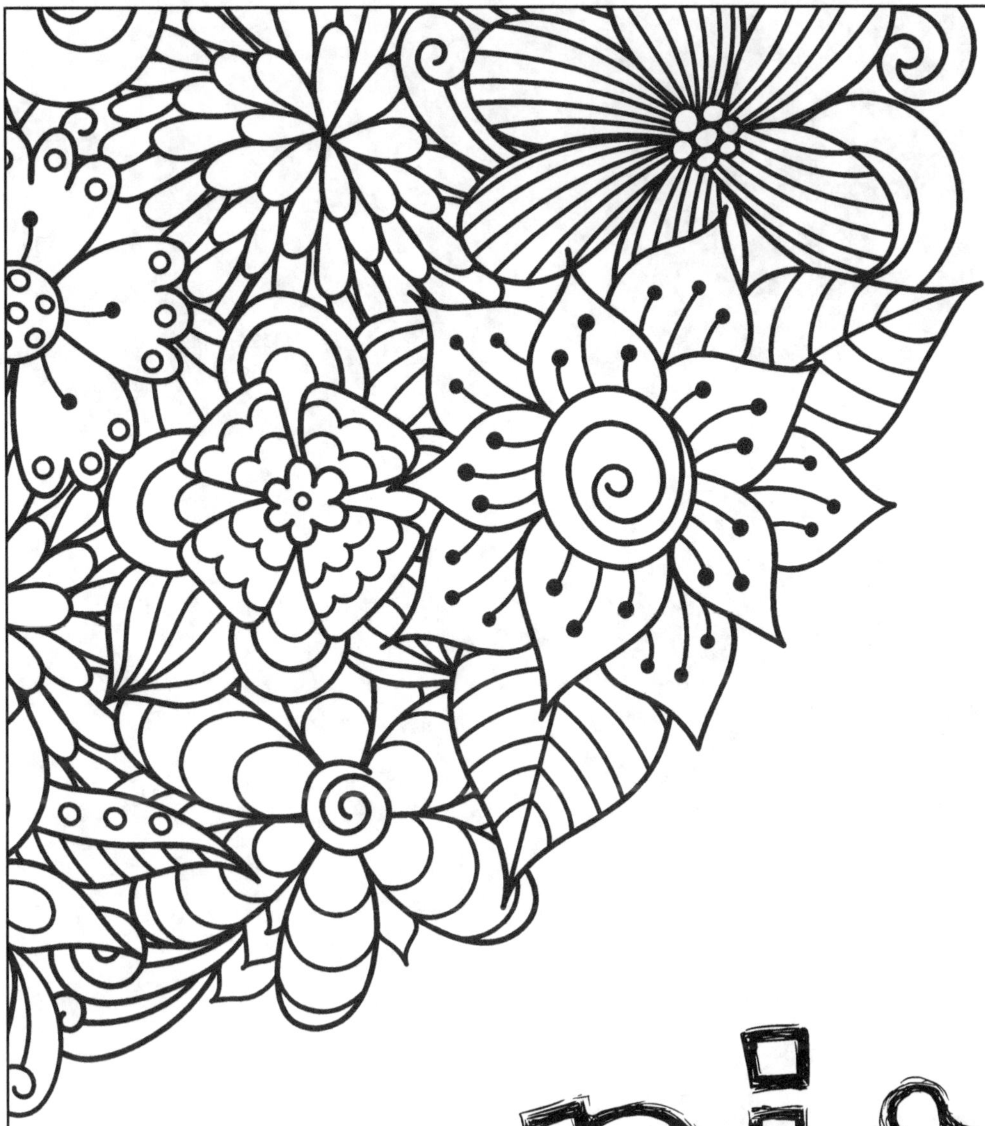

piss
off

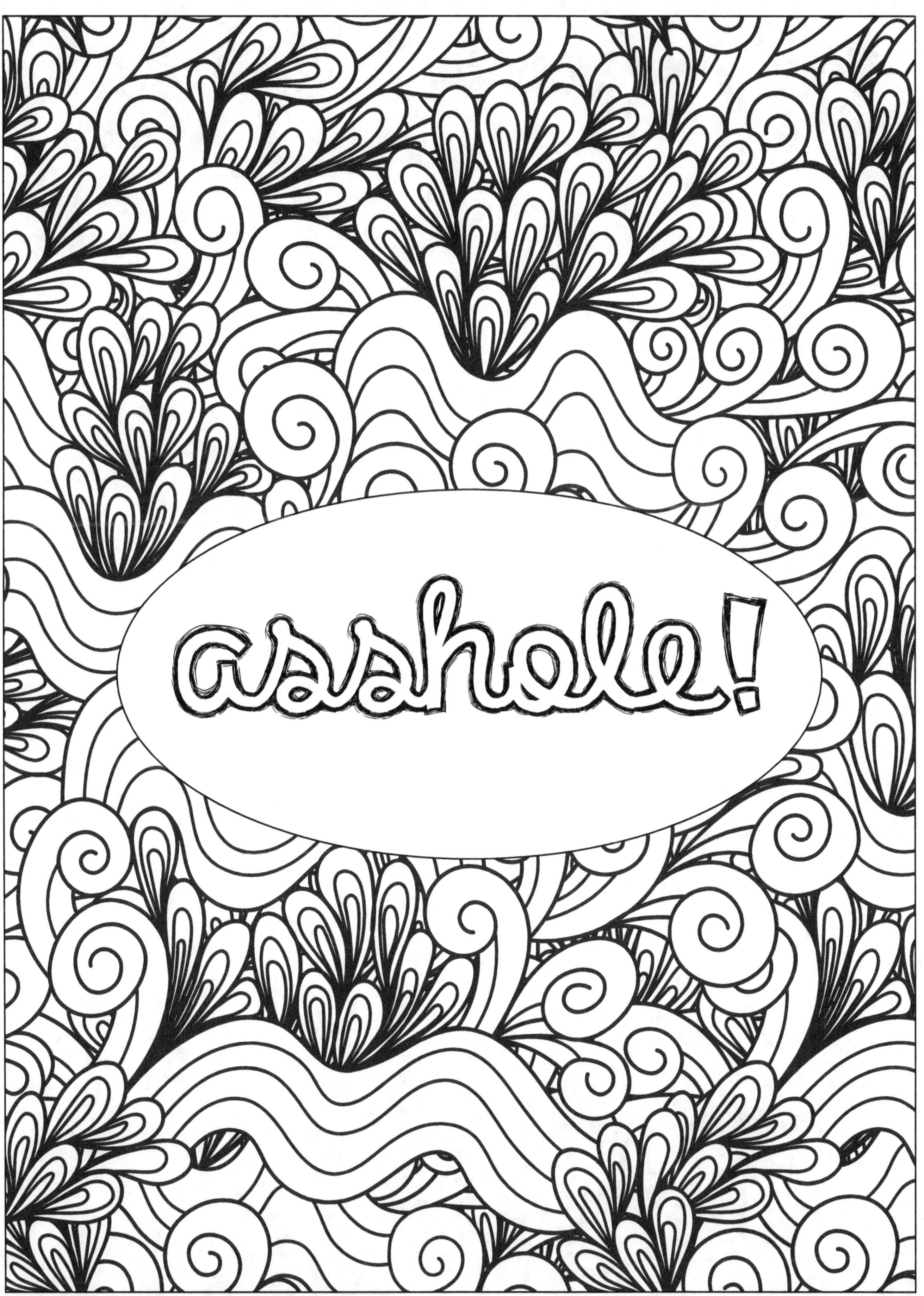
asshole!

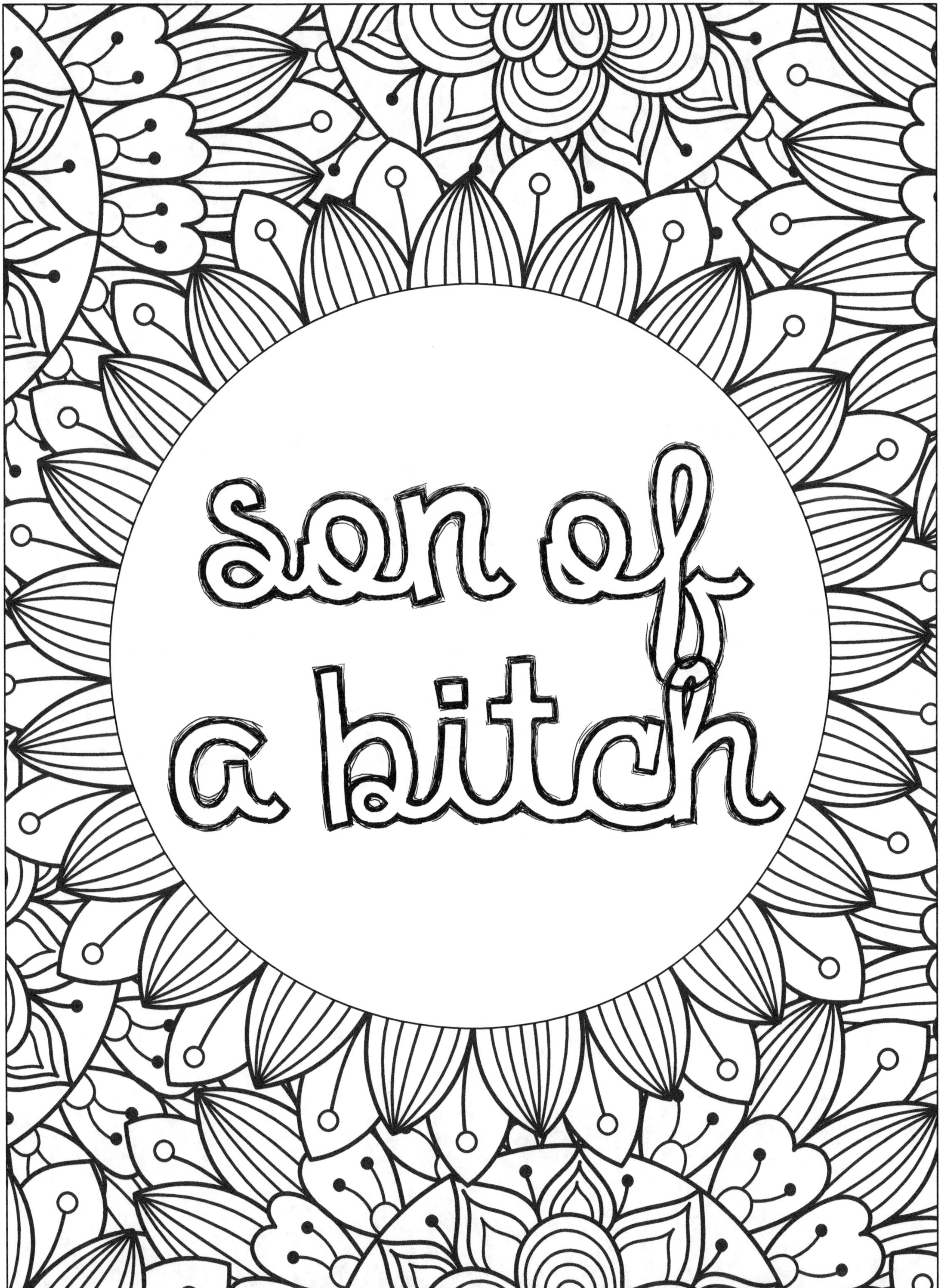
son of
a bitch

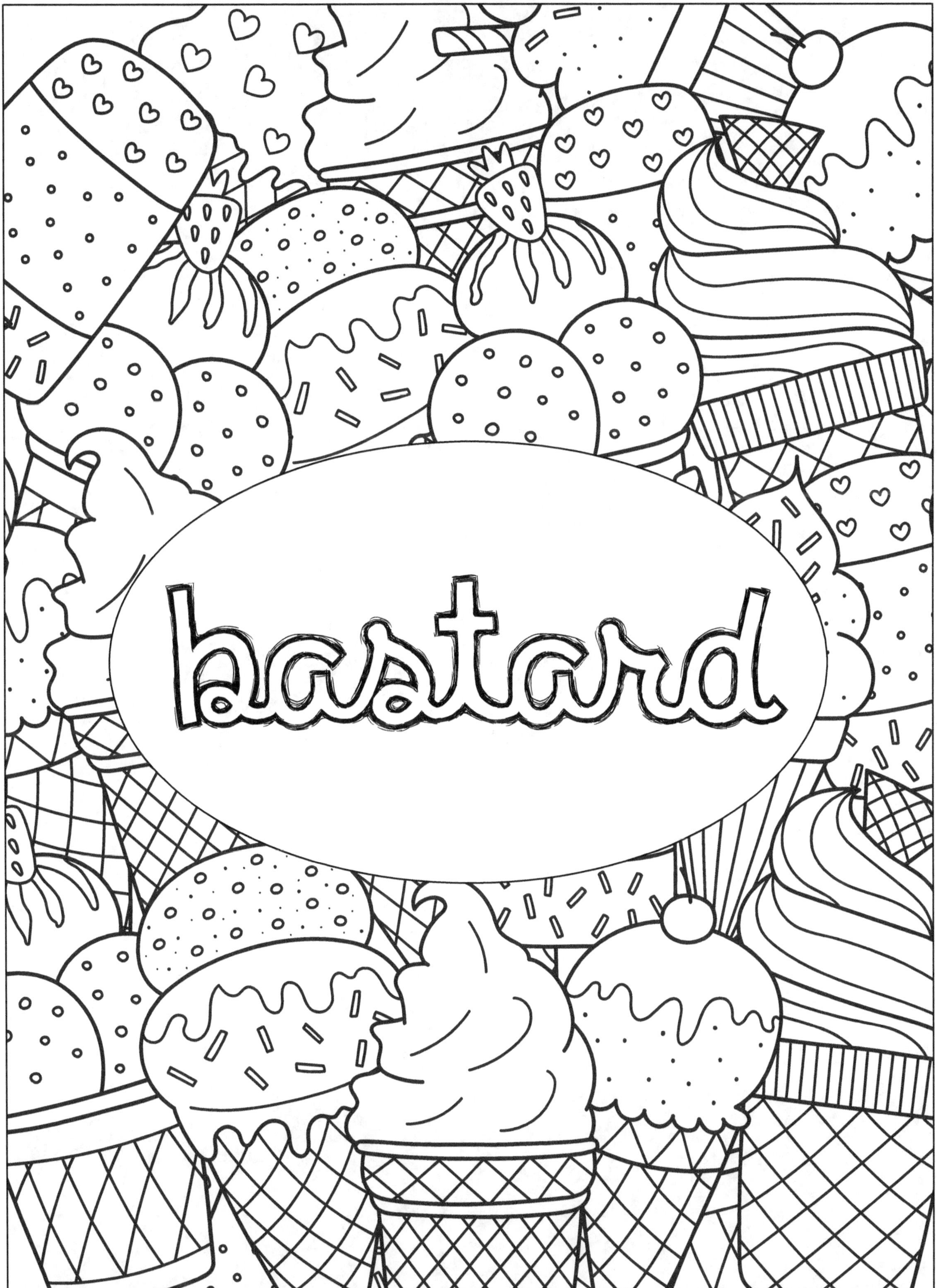
bastard

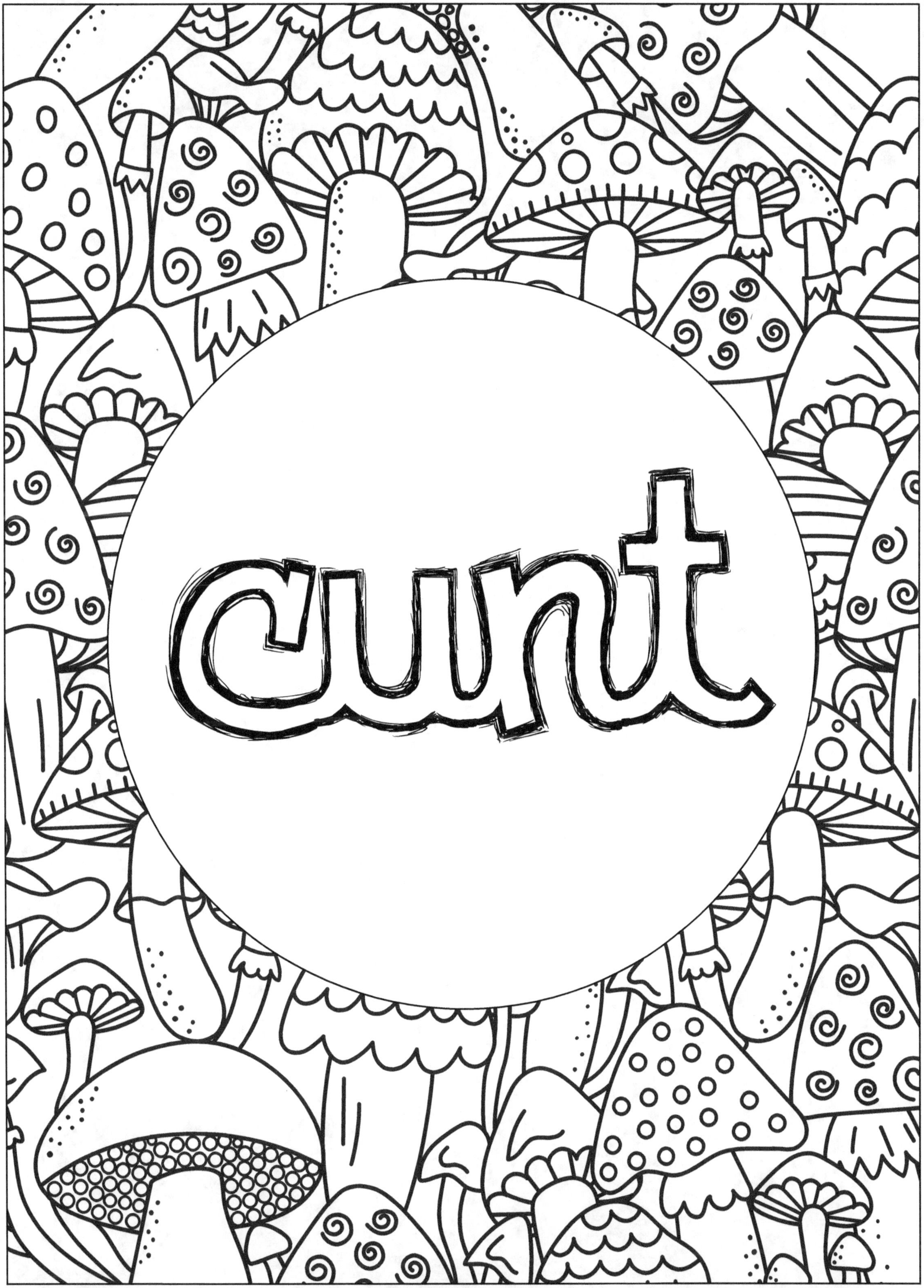
cunt

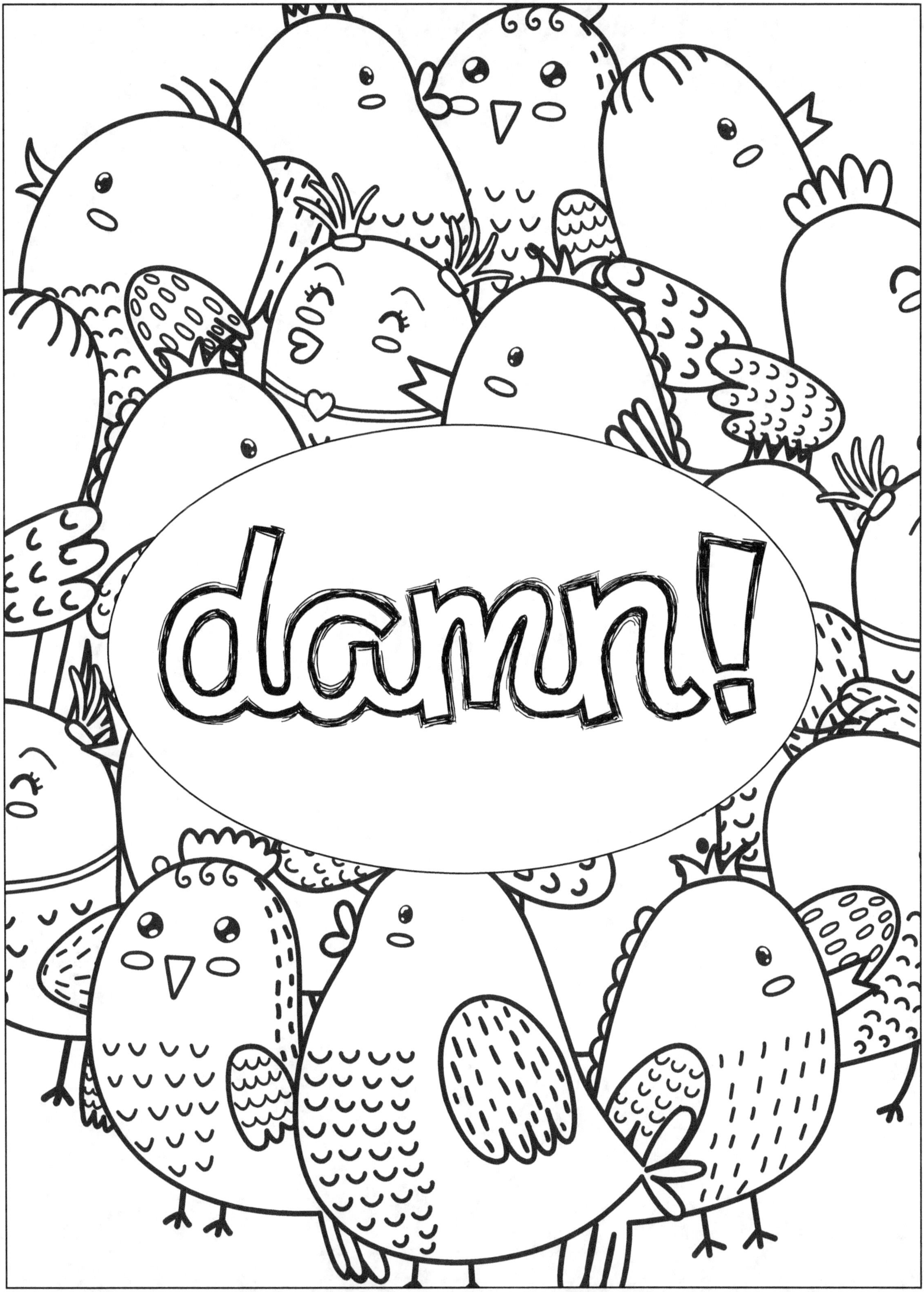
damn!

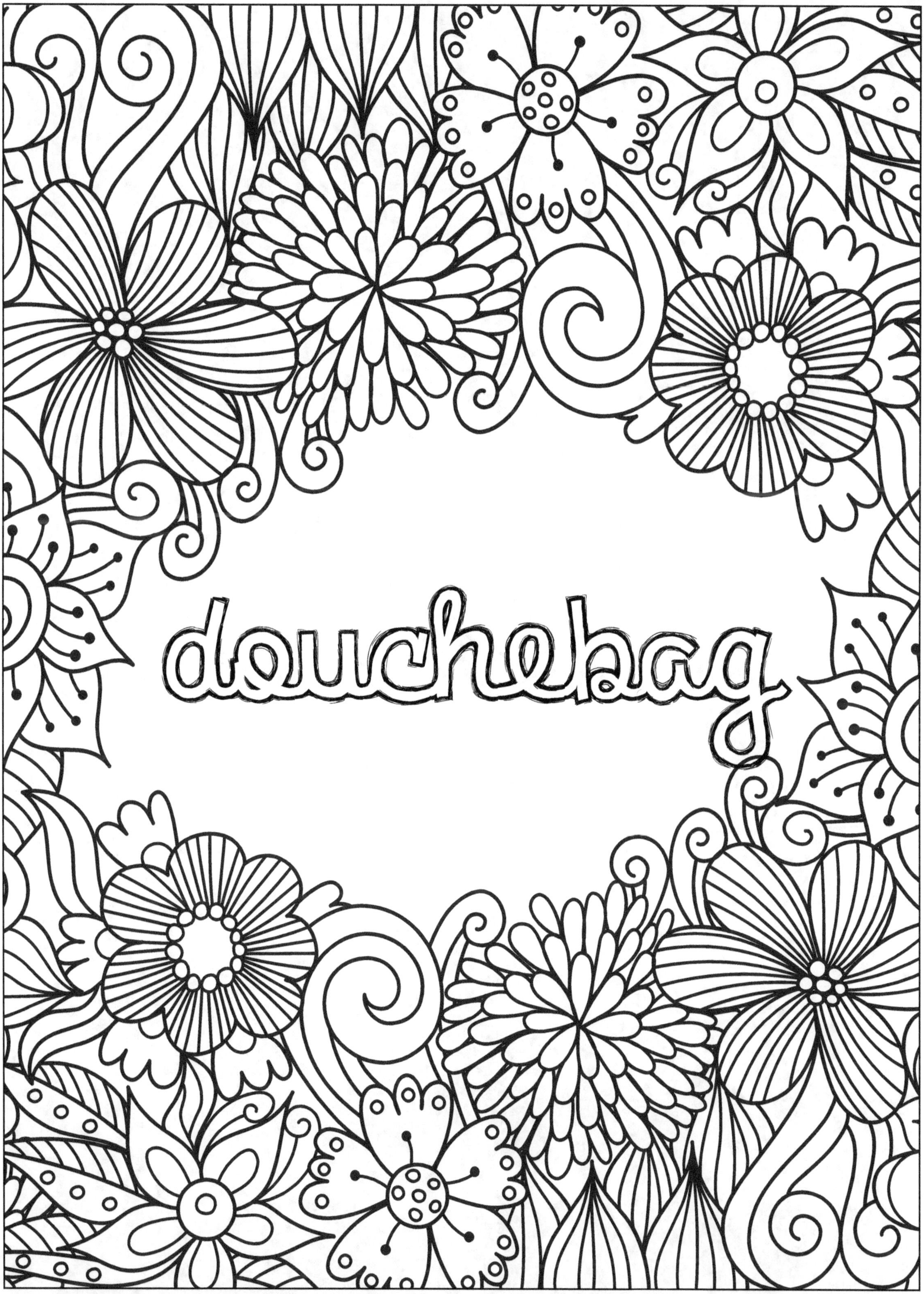
douchebag

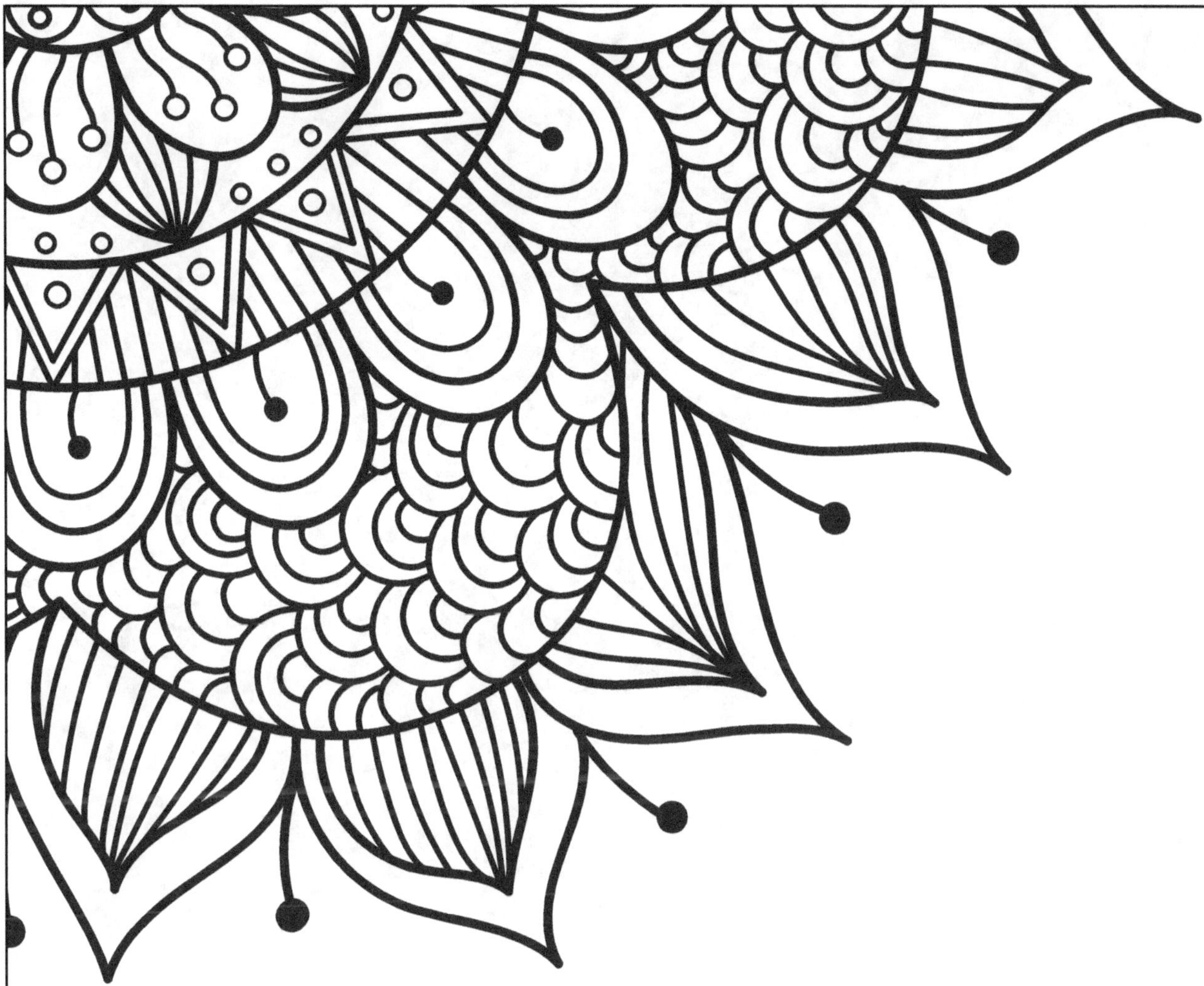

bitch

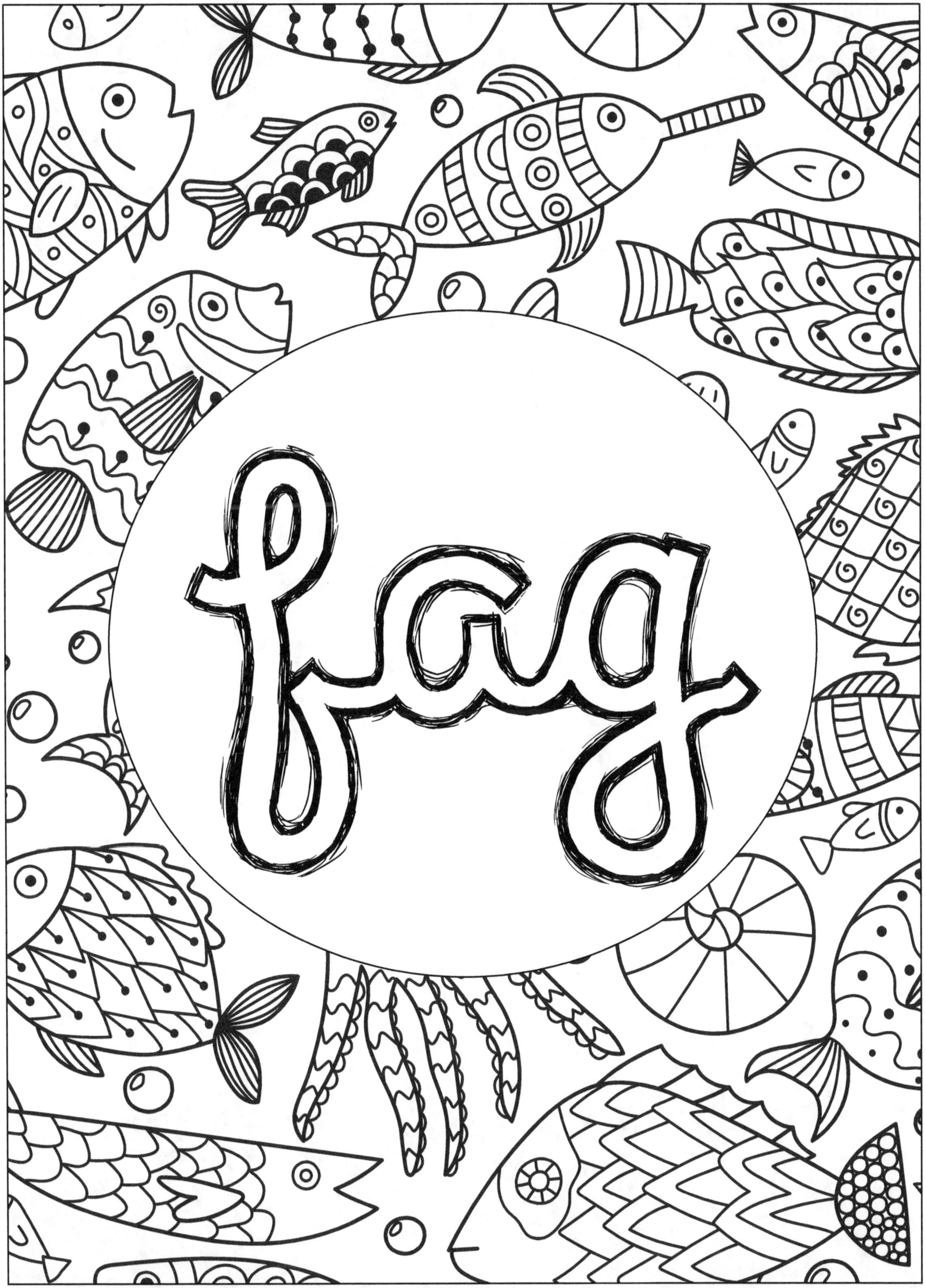
fag

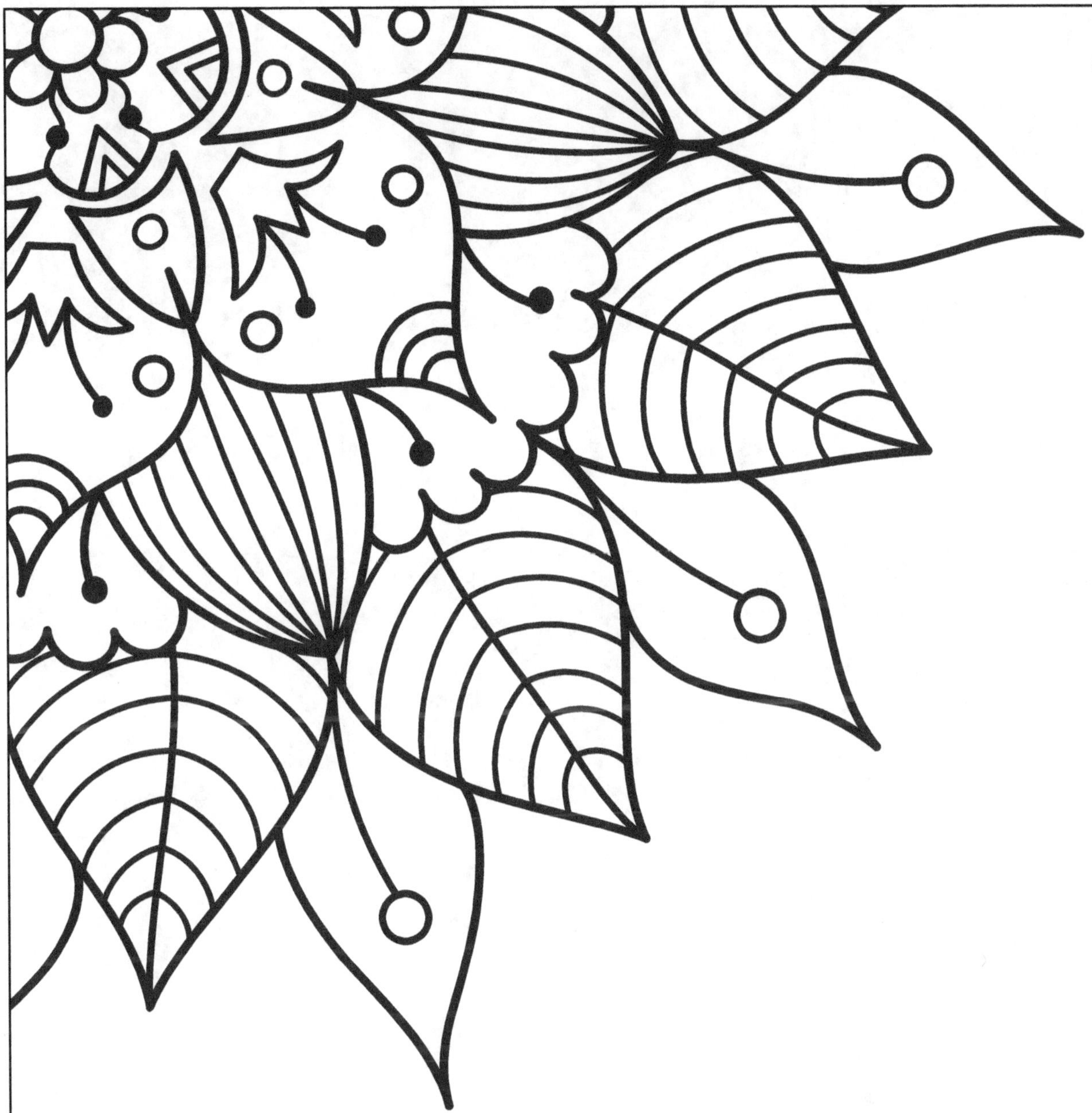

whore!

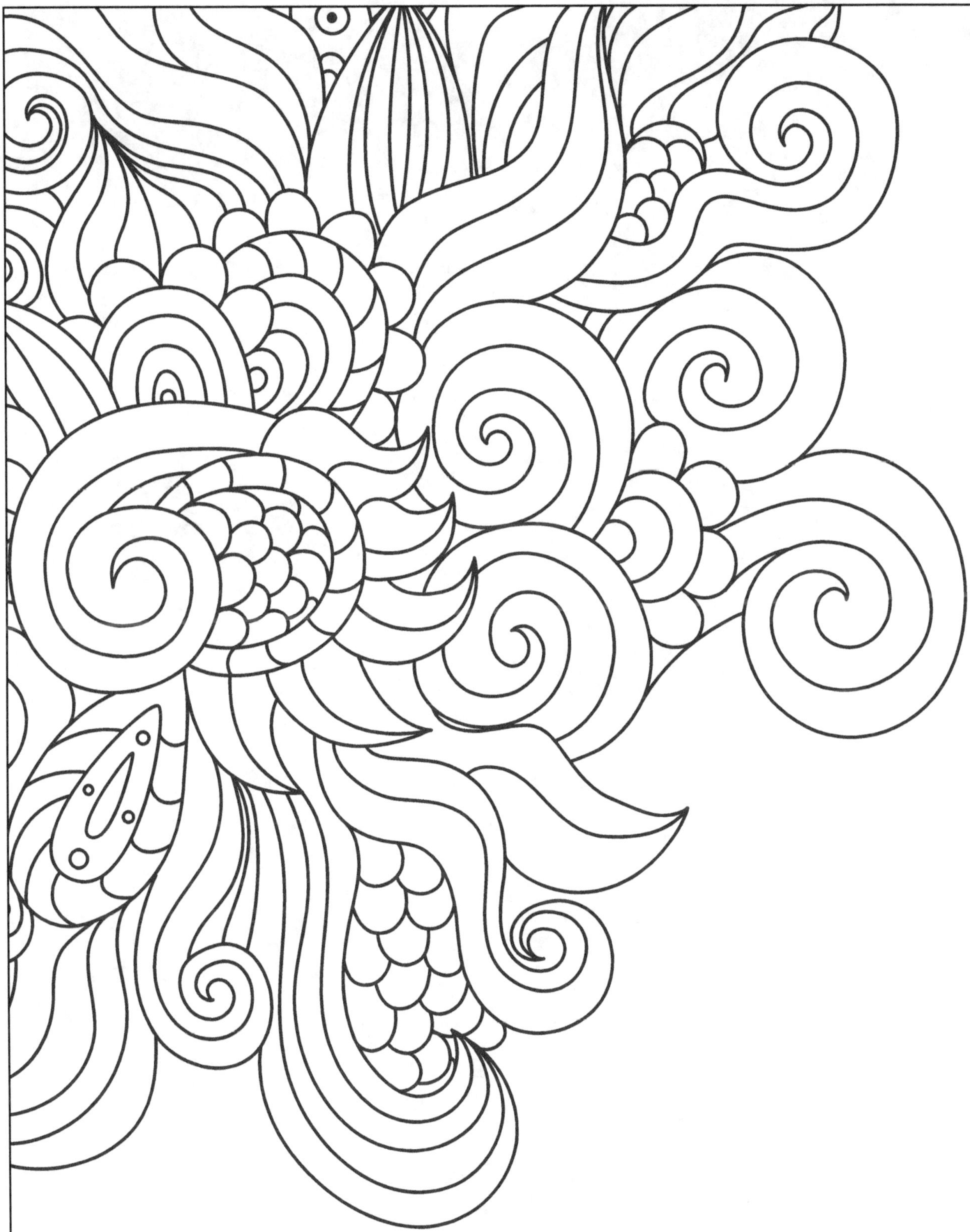

jerkoff!

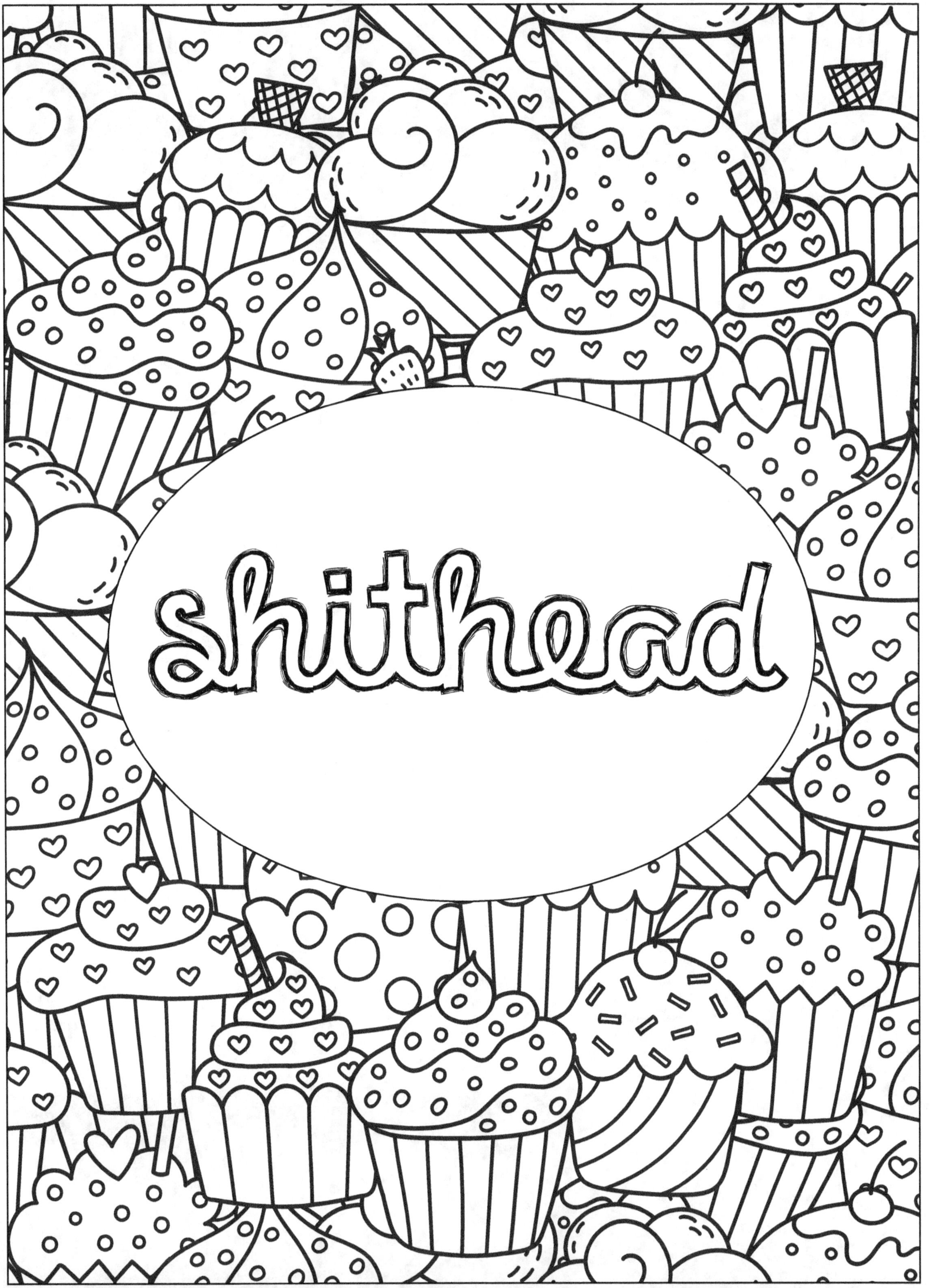
shithead

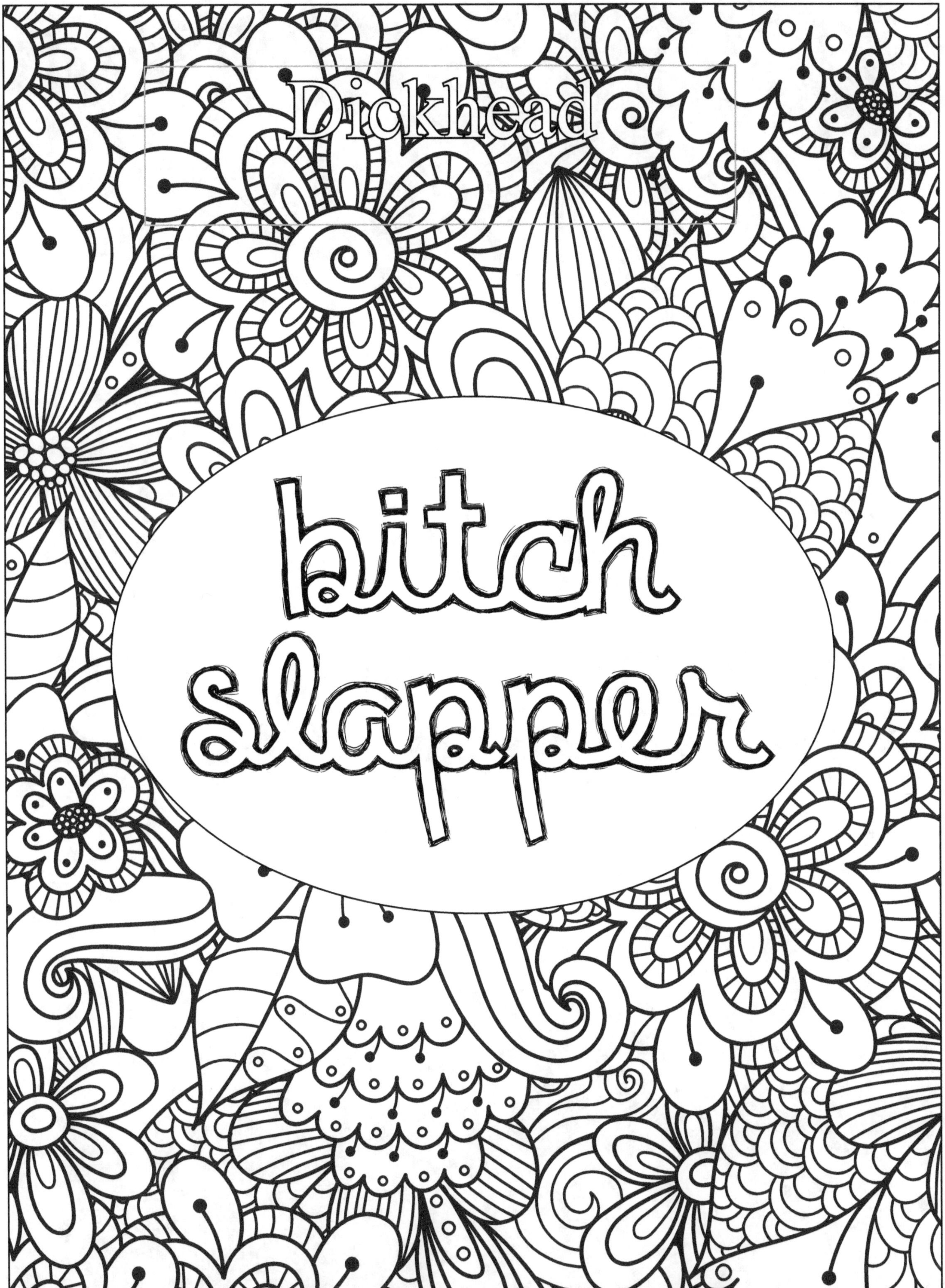
Dickhead
bitch slapper

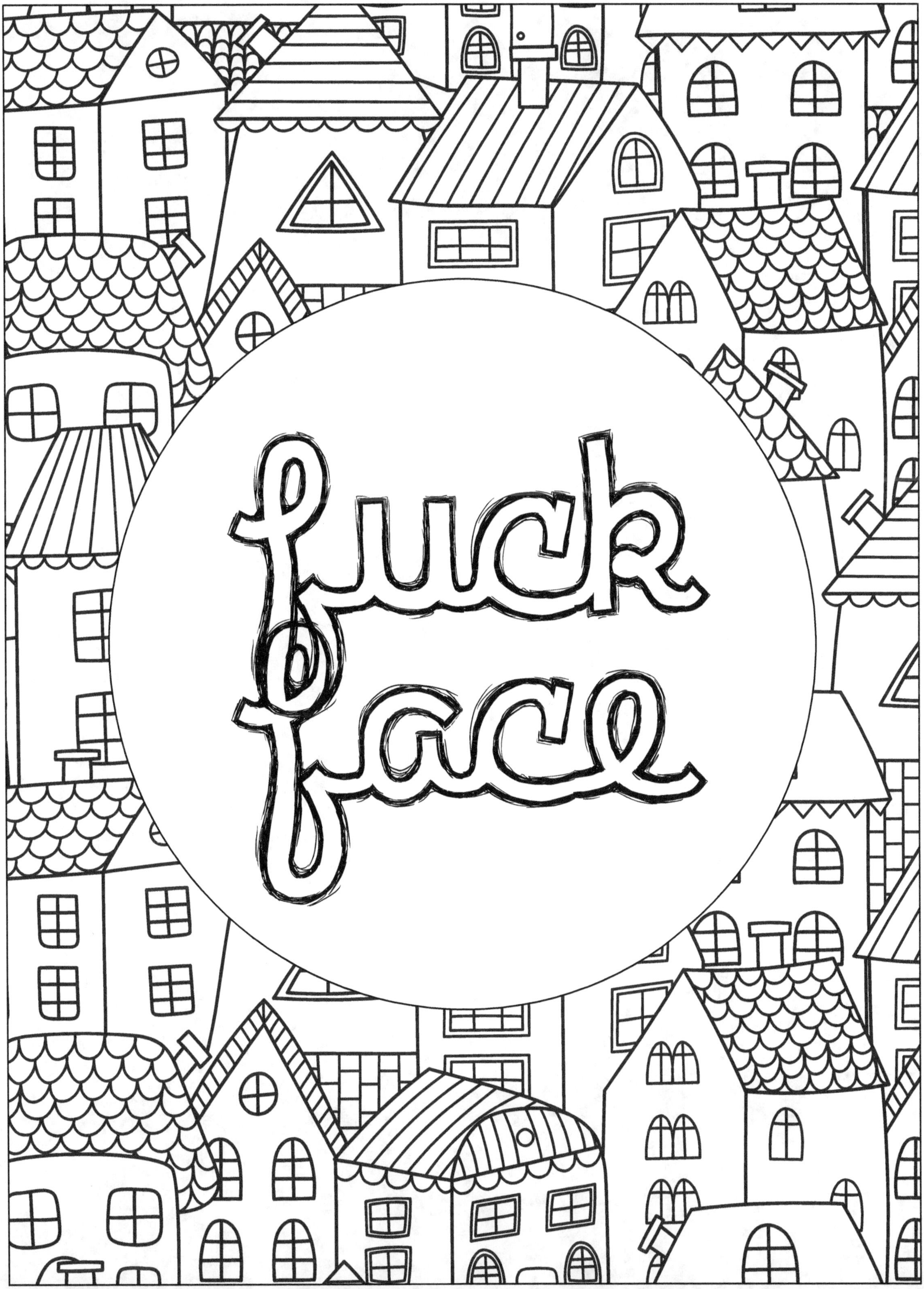
fuck face

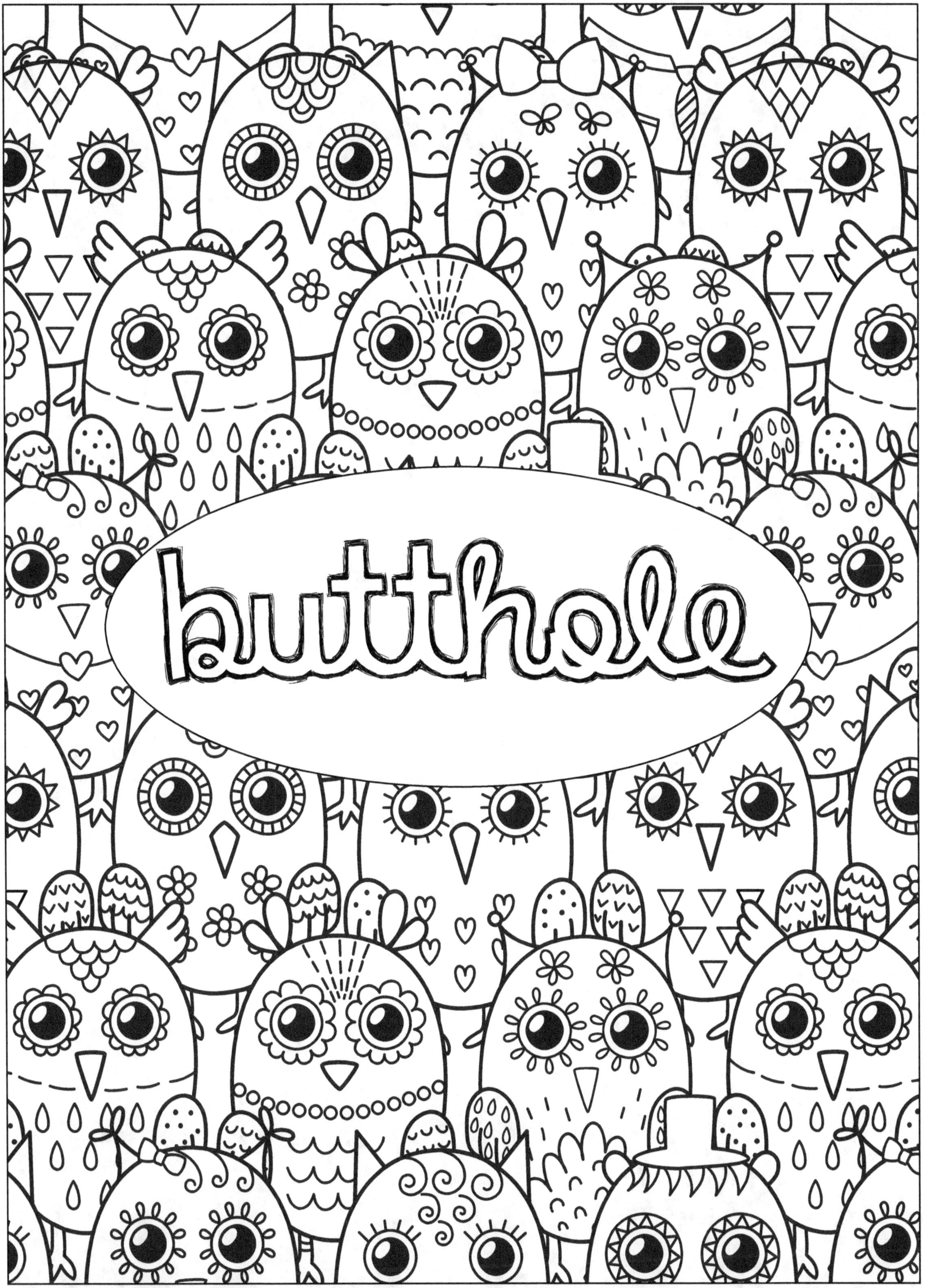
butthole

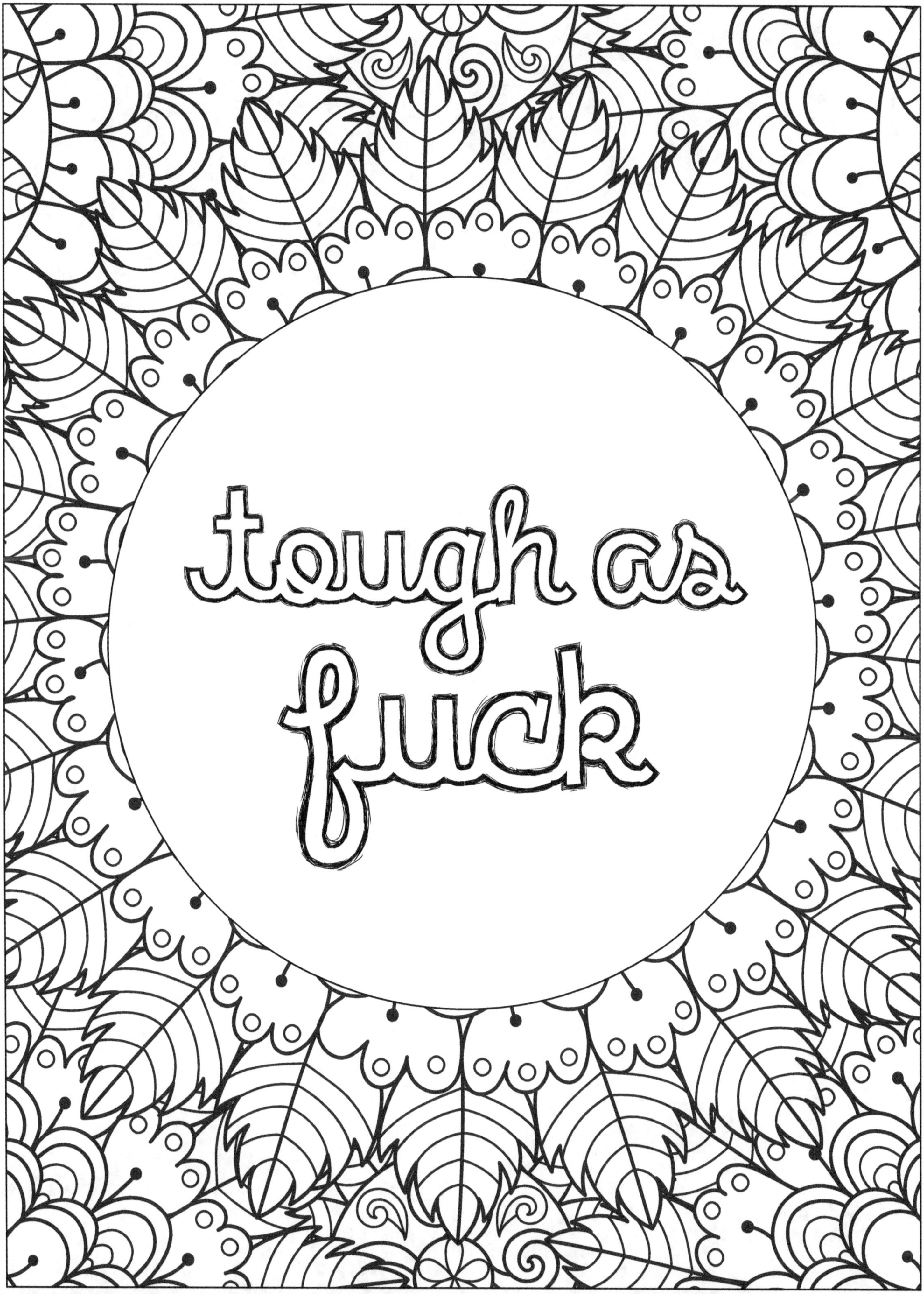
tough as fuck

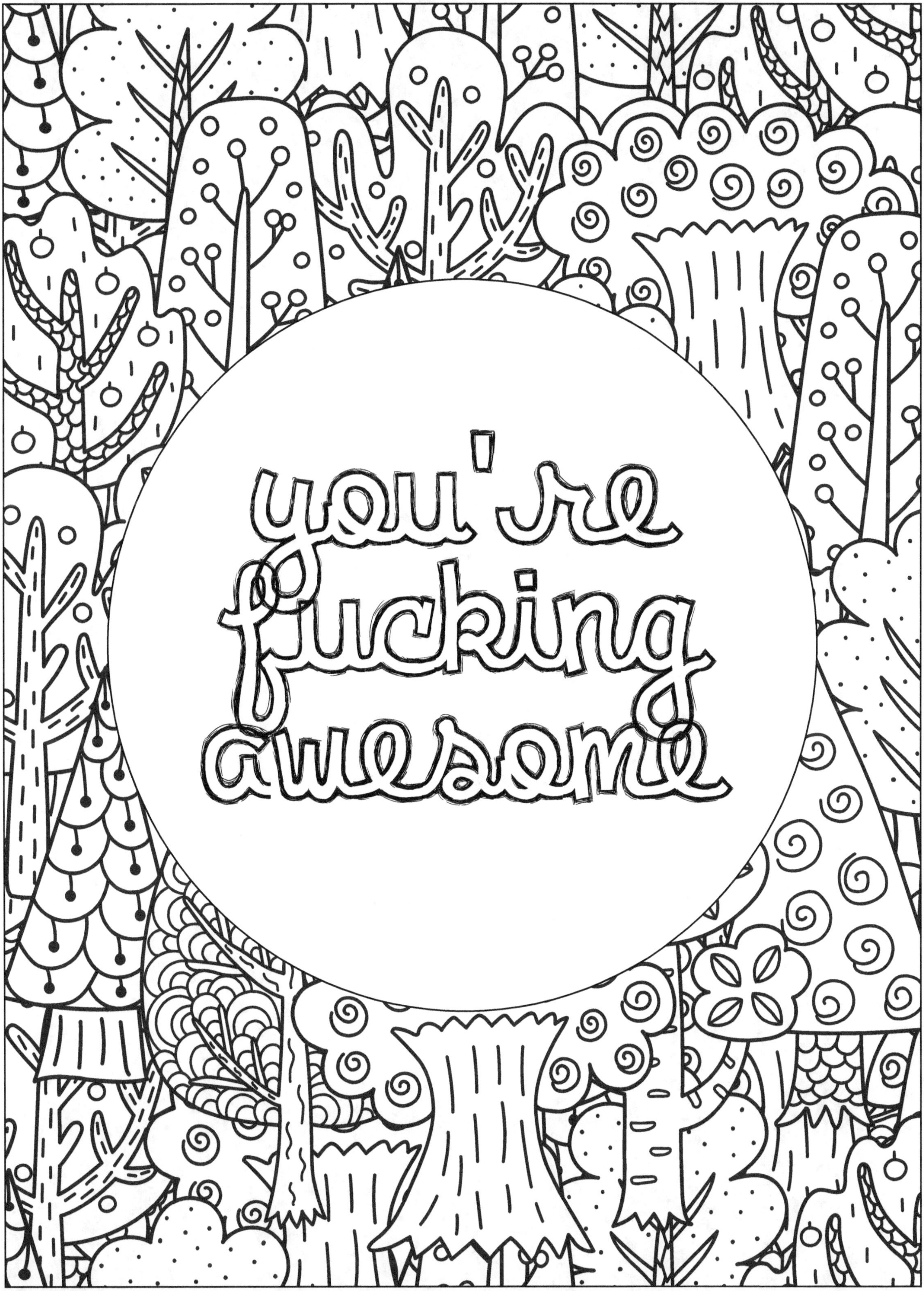
you're fucking awesome

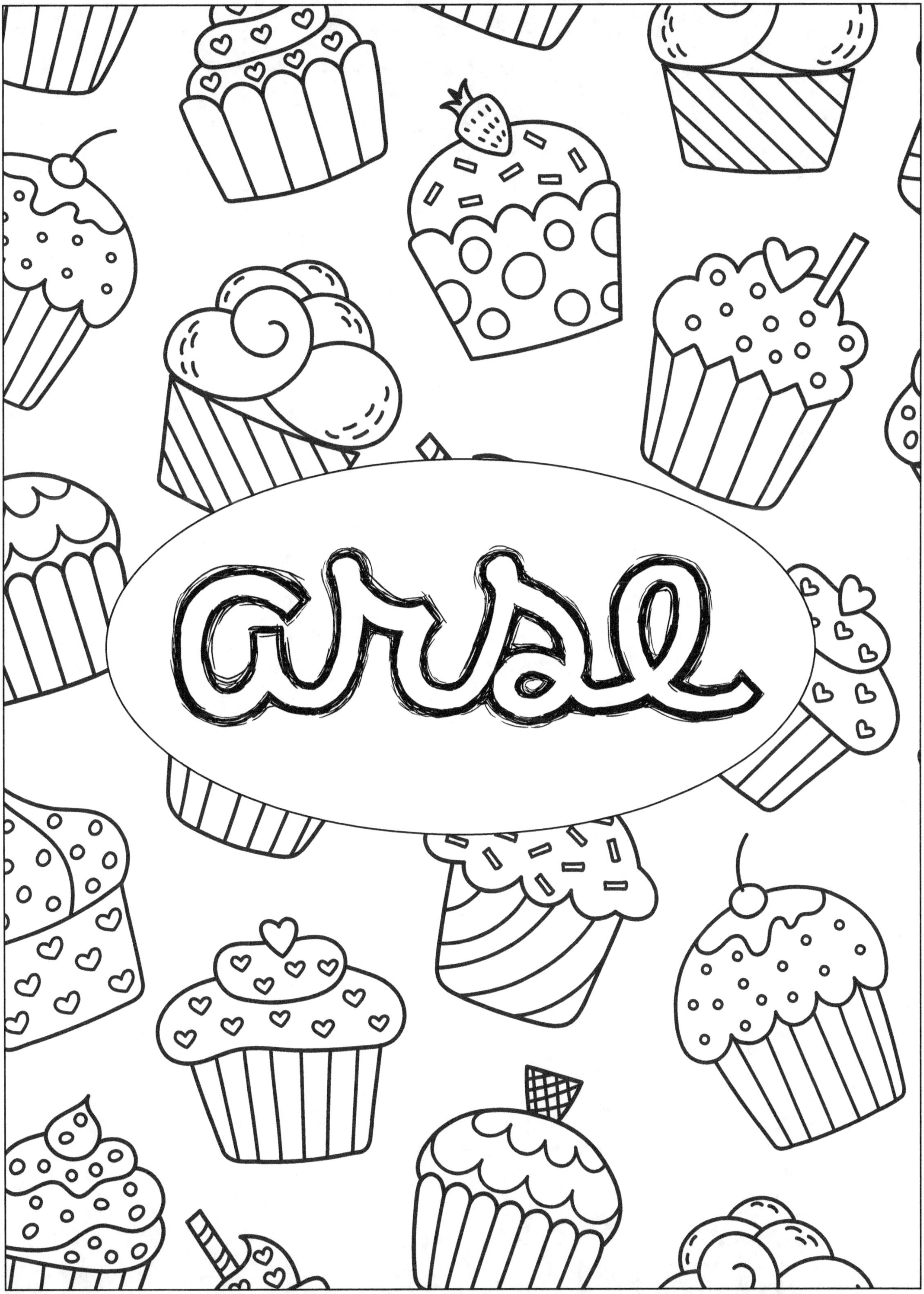
arse

ballsucker

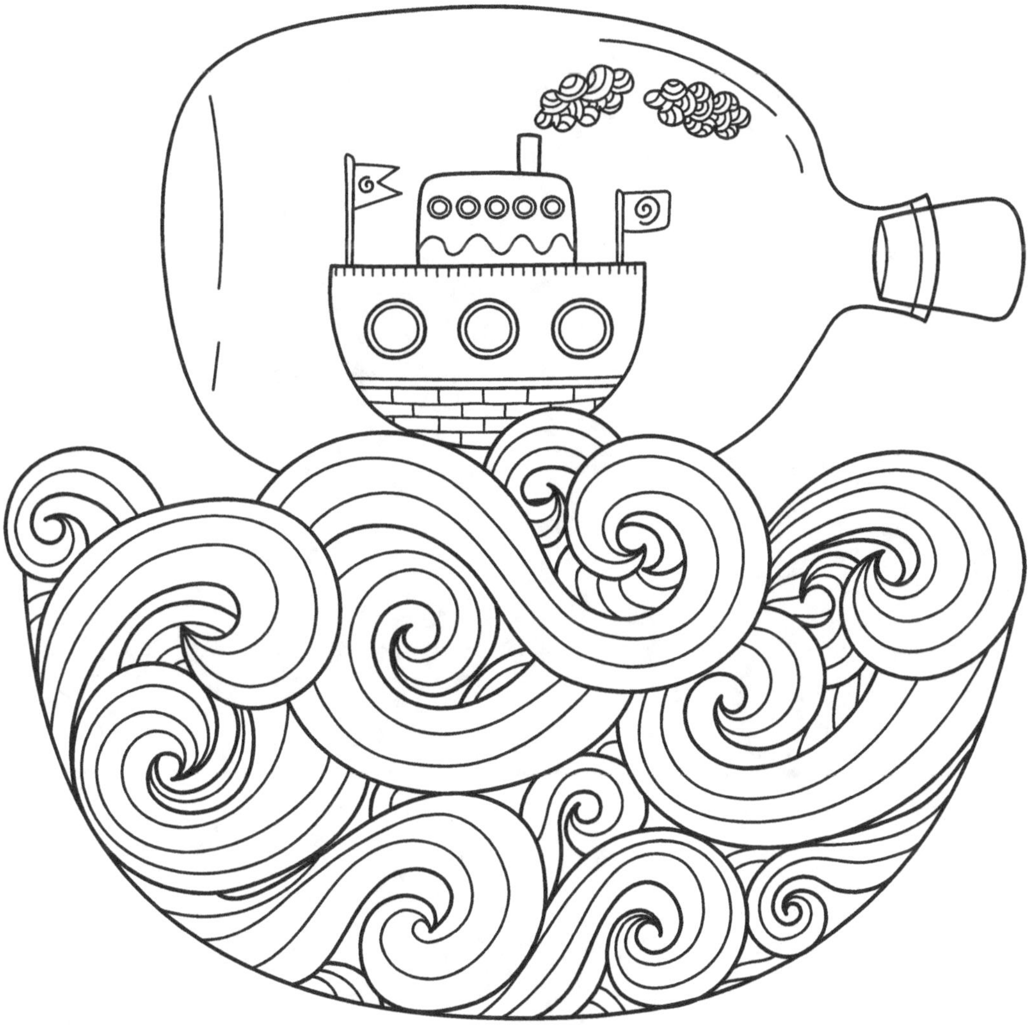

faceass

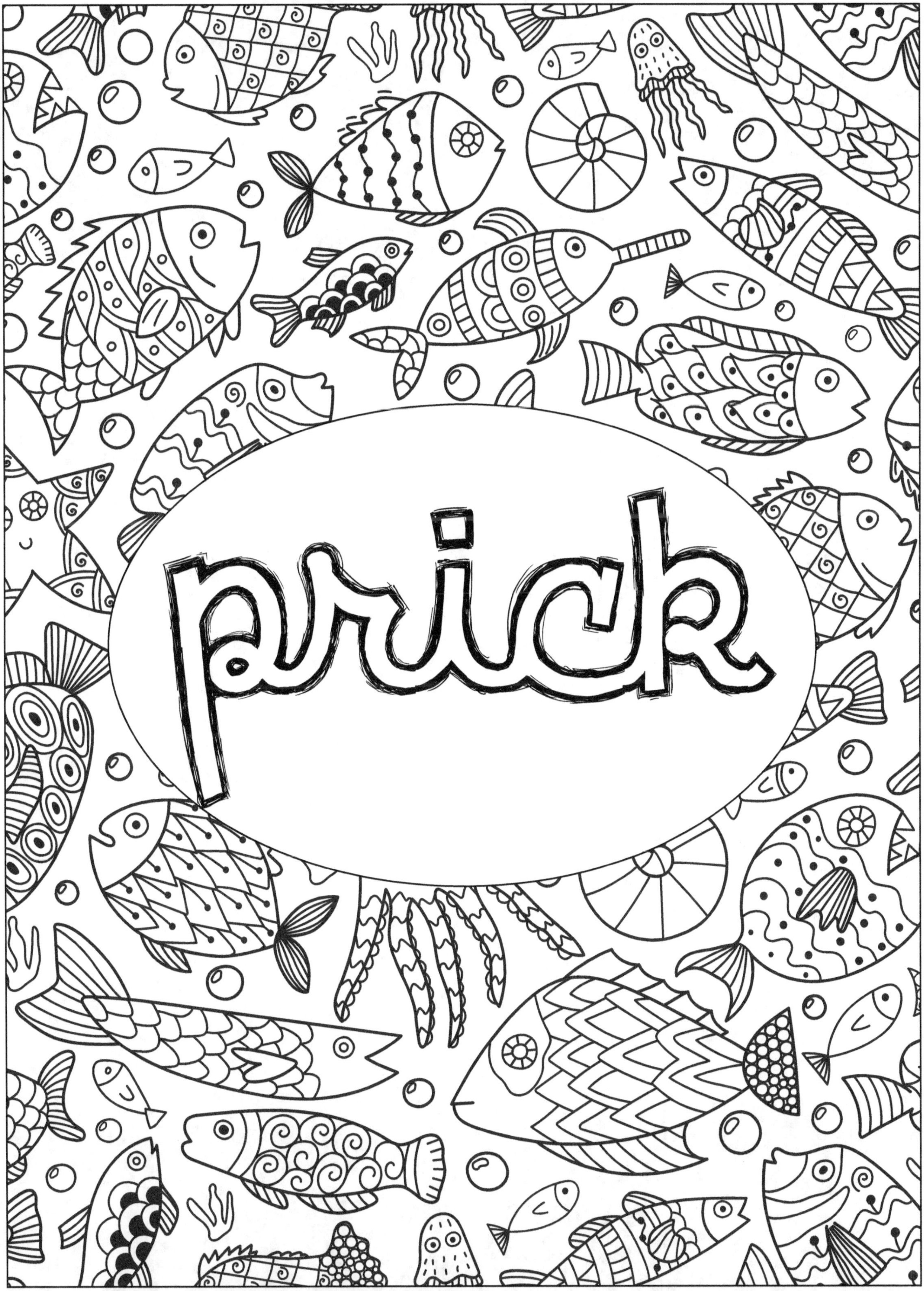
prick

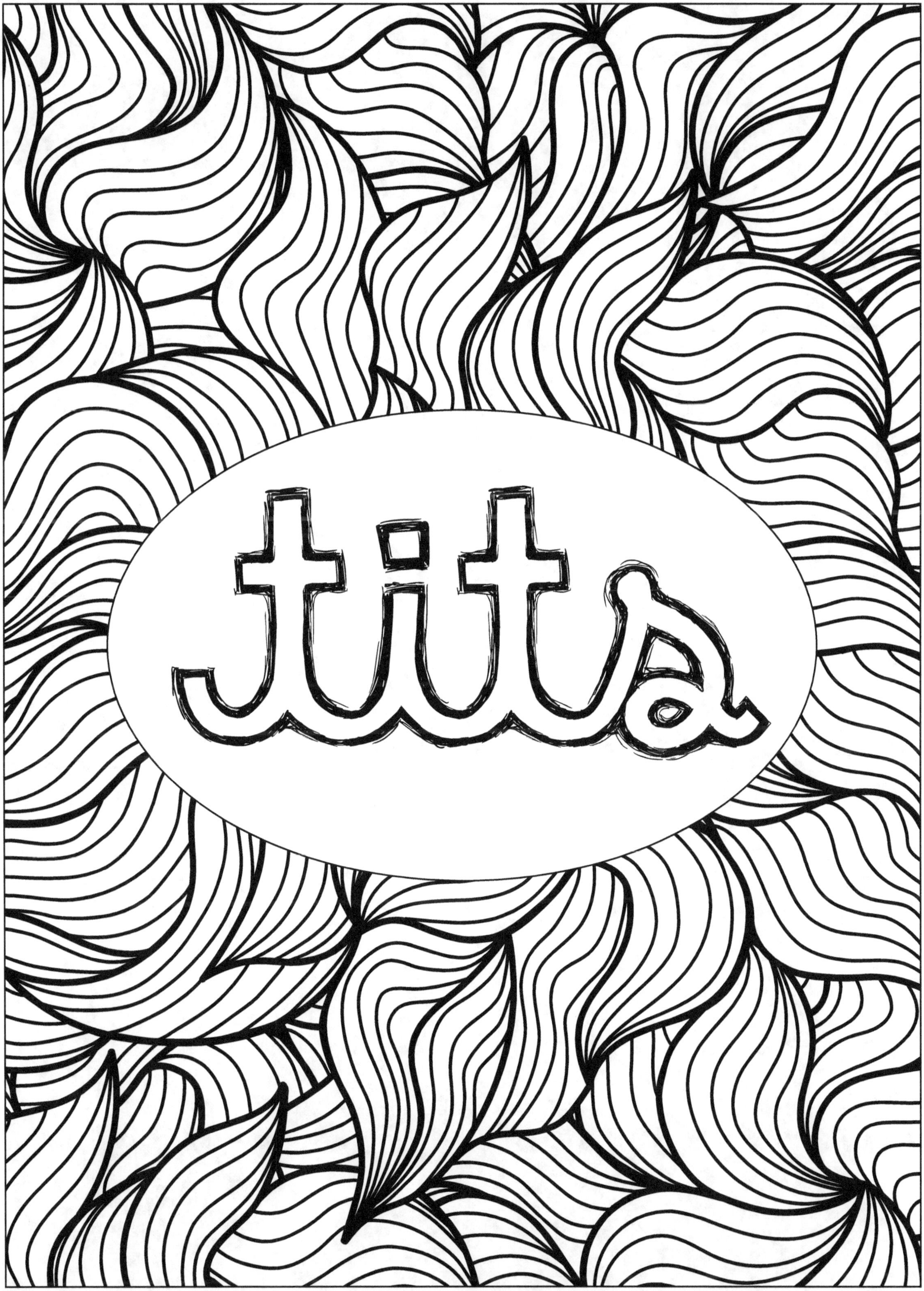
tits

www.ingramcontent.com/pod-product-compliance
Lightning Source LLC
Chambersburg PA
CBHW080849170526
45158CB00009B/2680
9781081280840